To Worship in Spirit and Truth

G-6521

To Worship in Spirit and Truth

A Liturgical Preparation Process for Pastoral Musicians and Liturgical Leaders

David Haas

GIA Publications, Inc.

Also by David Haas

*With Every Note I Sing: Prayers for Music Ministers
and Those Who Love to Sing*

*I Will Sing Forever: More Prayers for Music Ministers
and Those Who Love to Sing*

Chart on pages 21–22
Copyright © 2001
The Emmaus Center for Music, Prayer and Ministry
1595 Blackhawk Lake Drive, Eagan, MN 55122.
Used with permission. All rights reserved.

Cover illustration and layout: Robert Sacha
Book design and layout: Robert Sacha

Editing assistance: Helen Haas, Tom Backen

G-6521
Copyright © 2004
GIA Publications, Inc.
7404 South Mason Ave., Chicago, IL 60638.
International Copyright Secured. All Rights Reserved.
ISBN: 1-57999-380-X

Printed in the United States of America.

To my parents:
for their true love of music and the liturgy,
for their magnificent and lavish love of people,
for their most humble love of God,
and, most amazing,
for the most blessed love shown toward me, their son.
Thank you, Mom and Dad,
for sharing that love with me.

Table of Contents

Foreword viii

Acknowledgments x

Part 1: Liturgical Preparation: What Is It? 1

Part 2: Who Actually Prepares the Liturgy? 5

Part 3: A 10-Step Process for Liturgical Preparation 9

Postlude 19

Appendix A: The Structure of the Eucharist 21

Appendix B: Prayers for the Preparation Process 23

Appendix C: Resources for Further Reading and Study 27

Foreword

Since the Second Vatican Council transformed Catholic celebration of the liturgy in the 1960s, many books and articles have appeared on the market aimed at helping pastoral practitioners celebrate "with style and grace." Some impart a theological understanding of Catholic worship, others delineate the responsibilities and spirituality of individual liturgical ministries, while still others provide commentary on official documents, outlining their prescriptions for public worship.

To Worship in Spirit and Truth distills much of the wisdom in this plethora of publishing. Its signal contribution is to provide pastoral leaders and liturgical musicians with a ten-step process by which to prepare themselves and their communities for a particular celebration of the Eucharist. Especially to be applauded is David Haas's emphasis on engaging the scriptures appointed for the day as a key to the preparation process; after all, the liturgy is, in Huub Oosterhuis's evocative words, "the Bible proclaimed, sung, and played." Also helpful is the author's distinction (based on the work of Austin Fleming) between "planning" and "preparing for" the liturgy as well as his list of fundamental principles underlying the work of the liturgy preparation team.

While reading this booklet cannot substitute for an in-depth study of the liturgy (a study well facilitated by the author's extensive list of further resources), it does provide a vision of liturgical preparation, wise counsel about the formation of those charged with preparing the community's liturgy, and a practical checklist for those performing this important ministry. Priests, deacons, liturgical coordinators, lectors, extraordinary ministers of the Eucharist, pastoral musicians, and "people in the pew" all should find this to be a useful supplement in their liturgical formation.

– (Fr. Jan) Michael Joncas
University of St. Thomas
St. Paul, Minnesota
May 12, 2004

Acknowledgments

I want to thank all of the people at GIA Publications, Inc., especially Alec Harris, Bob Batastini, Michael Cymbala, Ed Harris, Kelly Dobbs-Mickus, Sarah Parker, Neil Borgstrom, Tom Hawley, and Rich Cruz for the tireless support and encouragement that they have given me over the years and still do so in friendship and with tremendous generosity. Special thanks also to Fr. Michael Joncas, Fr. Jim Bessert, and Fr. Edward Foley, who were among my first teachers in my study of the liturgy. I want to express my gratitude to Fr. John Fitzpatrick, Fr. Tom Krenik, Jan Viktora, and the late Michael Grimes, who were all part of the wonderful pastoral staff when I was Director of Music and Liturgy at St. Thomas Aquinas Church in St. Paul Park, Minnesota, from 1982–1985. During that time we served together as the liturgy preparation team for our parish community, and it was this experience that formed the beginnings of my convictions on liturgy and the processes found in these pages. The memories of those prayerful preparation meetings are still precious to me.

It is very important also to express my love and thanks to Fr. George DeCosta, Lori True, Fr. Ray East, Jim Moudry, Bill Huebsch, Joe Camacho, Fr. Paul Jaroszeski, Mary Werner, Fr. Bob Duggan, Vicky Tufano, Bonnie Faber, Mike Griffin, Tom Conry, Fr. Don Neumann, Jo Infante, and again to Fr. Jim Bessert for all that I have learned from them regarding liturgical preparation and sacramental practice as well as for their friendship and support. Much of their wisdom and many of their creative insights are woven into the content of this resource.

May God truly bless the living spirits and memories of Madelin Sue Martin, Fr. Jim Dunning, Ralph Kiefer, Fr. Eugene Walsh, and

Bishop Kenneth Untener, all who lavishly shared with so many the unending, treasured pearls of wisdom in regards to liturgy, liturgical preparation, and the formational power of communal sung prayer. Thanks to Helen Haas and my good friend Tom Backen for their generous help in editing my words, and to my dear friends and colleagues Kate Cuddy, Art Zannoni, Sr. Gertrude Foley SC, Leisa Anslinger, Tom Franzak, Sr. Kathleen Storms SSND, Stephen Petrunak, Rob and Mary Glover, Sr. Roberta Kolasa SJ, Tony Alonso, Rob Strusinski, Barbara Conley-Waldmiller, and Dan Kantor. Love and thanks to my parents, and finally, to my good friend Marty Haugen. Marty shared years ago the insight that as liturgical ministers we actually experience the liturgy *twice*—first when we plan, prepare, and rehearse, and second, when we actually pray and celebrate the liturgy with the believing community. May we always remember this and hold it close to our hearts.

—*David Haas*
May 20, 2004
The Ascension of the Lord

Part 1
Liturgical Preparation: What Is It?

Whenever any of us participate in a liturgical celebration that is well conceived, life-giving, and transformational, we know that it didn't just happen. It is usually the result of hard work, agonizing preparation, long rehearsals, and attention to detail. The Spirit does its work, but prior to any liturgical celebration, a good foundation must have already been laid and reflected upon.

As ministers of sung worship, we need skills and knowledge of the liturgy, its elements, and how music can help amplify and give strength to important ritual actions. In many parishes, the minister of music is the primary "planner" or "convener" of the group, whose responsibility it is to prepare the parish liturgies. More commonly, the parish minister of music does the planning all by him or herself. There are many magazines, journals, and other publications that give us musical suggestions and recommendations;

however, liturgy planning often becomes reduced to "picking out the songs" rather than an experience during which we pray, reflect, live, and celebrate the rituals and scriptures as a process for designing parish worship. As music ministers, liturgists, and pastors, we find ourselves fearful to be creative and imaginative and would rather just "get the task done," which results in merely "filling in the blanks," doing "the usual," and stifling the creativity of the Spirit, sometimes in order to be more "efficient."

While understandable, we need to challenge ourselves and our ministerial orientation regarding the precious nature and critical importance of good liturgical preparation and celebration anew. There is no magic recipe for good liturgy—only hard work, prayerful reflection, attentiveness, and care. Good liturgical celebration requires agonizing choices and a lot of sweat. Too often, decisions are left to chance. Details are put off to the last minute. And the path of least resistance seems to prevail. The acceptance of "good enough" should be anathema to us as liturgical leaders in our parish communities.

You will find no sample "liturgical planning" sheets in this book. That will be left to other books, magazines, and sources. They may be helpful, and there are plenty of different resources in that regard for you to choose from. It is a central premise of this book, however, that liturgical preparation requires much more than "filling in the blanks" and assigning roles and responsibilities. This guide is concerned with the deeper elements and concerns of preparation. Before we make specific choices and assign roles, we should be concerned with the work of the Spirit and of the heart. The primary elements are not what we may commit to paper but what we are willing to truly work toward and open ourselves to: quality, authentic, passionate, and faithful celebration that proclaims Jesus Christ as Lord and the Sunday Assembly as the Church, called to offer praise and lament and to surrender itself to conversion and mission. This means a commitment of time, talent, and priority.

A development and commitment to a strong liturgical preparation process is integral to our ministry of liturgical and musical leadership and is just as important (sometimes more so) as our choir rehearsals and other activities. The process presented in these pages has been tested in many parish settings and is by design collaborative, credible, doable, and helpful in creating and designing liturgical experiences. The process is thoughtful, imaginative, and authentic, yet still true to the desire of the liturgical books and their norms. Much of the vision for this process is inspired by the work of Austin Fleming and Mark Searle, both prophets and leaders in the important enterprise of liturgical preparation.[1]

Austin Fleming teaches us to remember that the liturgy, for the most part, is already "planned." Its structure is in place and does not need much change on our part. The foundational elements are already there—present and rich. What we are called to do is shape and *prepare* these elements. Our call is to "fine-tune," focusing the ritual and bringing it to life "off the page." Preparing a liturgy is more than filling in "slots" on a form or just picking out songs and specific prayers. Responsible liturgical preparation challenges us to keep the Paschal Mystery of the death and resurrection of Christ at the center of all communal prayer and to recognize that the entire liturgical year and each liturgical celebration is a celebration of that great mystery. Liturgical preparation always remembers, reverences, and seeks out the full and attentive participation of the gathered assembly. Liturgical preparation asks us to consider and examine the entire ritual experience, to identify key ritual moments, actions, gestures, sounds, and other aspects that will charge the community to celebrate their faith in a way that is authentic and, hopefully, always pointed toward conversion.[2]

A basic understanding of the liturgy, its structure, spirituality, and movement as well as the "high" and "low" points of the ritual action is a fundamental necessity when engaged in preparation.[3] With a clear understanding of the role of the assembly, liturgical principles, the role of music in ritual, and the renewed order of the liturgy, we can truly prepare and design a worship experience that is sound and, at the same time, creative and life-giving. The stakes are high, as so eloquently expressed by our bishops: "Faith grows when it is well expressed in celebration. Good celebrations foster and nourish faith. Poor celebrations may weaken and destroy it."[4]

Notes:

1. Dr. Searle's *Liturgy Made Simple* (Collegeville: Liturgical Press) is an excellent introduction to the deep structures of the liturgy, providing a good foundation for sound planning. *Preparing for Liturgy* (Chicago: Liturgy Training Publications) by Austin Fleming is a very important basic resource for anyone engaged in liturgical preparation.

2. These principles are explored more deeply in *The Ministry and Mission of Sung Prayer* (Cincinnati: Saint Anthony Messenger Press).

3. Appendix A illustrates the Order of Mass with a clear understanding in this regard.

4. Music in Catholic Worship, Bishops' Committee on the Liturgy, United States Conference of Catholic Bishops, 1972, n. 6.

Part 2

Who Actually Prepares the Liturgy?

Who are the people preparing liturgies? First of all, remember that there are basically two types of liturgical preparation: 1) seasonal or long-range preparation and 2) preparation for a specific liturgical celebration. Many parishes have a liturgy or worship committee, which is an important group to have in place to direct the vision of the parish's liturgical life and to evaluate and plan for the future. This committee should be engaged in a long-range seasonal vision and have stated priorities, but it is not the group that should be preparing any specific liturgy. The parish liturgy committee is a large group of people that is most successful when concerned with the *overall* liturgical and prayer life of the community. In other words, they are more of a visionary group. Their charge is to name and set liturgical policies, provide the tone for and evaluate major feasts and seasons, and offer more general direction to the parish staff and community at large. This is by no means a diminishment of their role, but rather, quite the contrary. This group needs to read, study, and explore the deeper dimensions of the parish liturgical life, set a course, and make larger, long-range decisions that truly affect the direction of liturgy in the parish.

The Liturgy Preparation Team

The process presented here proposes that a smaller, more focused group of people take on the task of setting the direction for the actual nuts and bolts of liturgical preparation, especially for specific celebrations. While not always possible, this group should include the priest who will preside at the parish liturgies. The music director, or person who is responsible for making musical choices, should obviously be there; if there is a liturgist who is someone other than the director of music, he or she should be present as well. It is also good to have two or three people from the parish community representing some diversity in age and/or cultural groupings involved. Using this model, there are five to six people at most who should be willing to meet weekly. This team of people would make an ongoing commitment to this ministry of preparation and thereby develop a connection with each other and the parish community in addition to growing in their understanding of their roles as ministers. Some parishes like to "rotate" people into such a group, and this often causes problems. It is best to have a stable group of people that is truly committed to doing this over a period of time, during which they will experience ongoing growth and competence in their work. The priest should be present at this meeting as his role is obviously a central part of the entire liturgical experience; however, he does not necessarily have to be the leader of the group. In many parishes, the priest is not able or is unwilling to participate. If this is the case, the process presented still offers a beginning path that the pastoral musician and other liturgical leaders will hopefully find valuable.

Forming the Liturgy Preparation Team

Far too often, people who participate in liturgical preparation may not be properly equipped to the task, even though their enthusiasm and willingness is high. It cannot be stressed enough that ongoing in-services, reading, and other formational activities are essential for a group charged with such an important task. While there are many resources available, obviously a good starting point would be to begin to delve into some of the basic liturgical documents.[1] Everyone needs to grasp the basic principles and foundations of liturgical celebration and to center on better participation in this ministry of liturgical preparation. While there is no substitute for a systematic study of the liturgy, some fundamental principles should always be at the center as we take part in the preparation of the liturgy.

1. **Liturgy is a celebration of faith.** While the liturgy is certainly a springboard for ongoing formation and conversion, it is *not* a classroom or catechetical session—it is a communal event during which a believing community gives voice to its faith and praise and celebrates Jesus Christ present among us.

2. **There is no "theme" for the liturgy, except the ongoing proclamation of the Paschal Mystery.** Regardless of the season or celebration, every time we gather to pray we celebrate and proclaim our dying and rising in Christ.

3. **The liturgy is an action of the assembly.** Liturgy is not an exercise of private prayer or personal devotion, nor is it a performance we attend to gain mere inspiration. It is the "work of the people," the gathered community, through Christ, with Christ, and in Christ. Every decision we make as liturgical and musical leaders should take this into account.

4. **Liturgy involves a rich diversity of ministries.** High-quality worship involves a rich diversity of people and their many gifts. The priest is the primary leader of prayer, but the gifts and talents of so many more are needed: lectors, eucharistic ministers, ministers of music, hospitality ministers, dancers, people who prepare the environment, sacristans, servers and, of course, those who actually prepare the liturgy.

5. **Liturgy is ritual prayer.** This means it utilizes a language and pattern of symbols, repetition, and an order that is communal, not the devotion of individuals.

6. **The liturgy is sung.** There is no such thing as a "quiet" or "silent" Mass. The liturgy is lyrical in nature, so the quality and role of liturgical music is vitally important because it is the primary language of such ritual activity and the central vehicle for participation of the assembly.

7. **Liturgy is concerned with ongoing conversion and mission.** In other words, the goal and purpose of the liturgy is not liturgy. Rather, it is a celebration of praise and lament, when the community is compelled to speak, touch, sing, and act in God's name for the life of the world. Nurturing disciples and sending us all forth on our mission is the ultimate aim, as expressed in the final challenge: "Go in peace to love and serve the Lord."

Notes:

1. See Appendix C, which provides many suggestions of books and resources for liturgical education and formation, a critical, ongoing part of the liturgy preparation team's work.

Part 3

A 10-Step Process for Liturgical Preparation

What follows is a prayerful, 10-step process that has proven to be helpful in preparing specific liturgical celebrations. The actual preparation meeting should take place early in the week, and after it becomes comfortable and familiar to the team should not take any longer than 90 minutes.[1] The team should have these basic and essential materials at their disposal: at least one copy each of the Lectionary, the Sacramentary, and parish hymnals or other primary music resources. The environment for the meeting should be informal. All should be seated in a circle, either around a table or in a more comfortable, "living room" type of atmosphere. A lighted candle is a nice centering piece for the meeting.

It is important to remember that the purpose of this process is not to produce a "script" of the liturgical celebration, a final plan to be "set in stone." Rather, the goal of this time is to provide a context and a basic direction for the priest, liturgist, and pastoral musician to "tweak" and finalize later. The final decisions and deliberations should take place after this meeting when the wisdom and insights from the preparation team have been pondered.

The Liturgical Preparation Process: 10 Steps

1. Prepare for the meeting.

Prior to the meeting, each member of the team should take some time to read and pray over the scriptures for the upcoming celebration and possibly even read a commentary on those readings.[2] Some preparatory reading and reflection before coming together only enriches the process. The music minister needs to do some initial exploration of music choices and come to the meeting with a draft of a musical lineup as a starting point. The homilist should do some preparatory work and reflection beforehand as well so he or she can offer to the group process.

It also would be good for the team members to ponder some initial questions that might serve as a backdrop for the preparation meeting, such as:

- What are the conditions under which this celebration will be taking place?
- Who will be there? (age groups, cultural groupings, economic distinctions)
- What are the potential "clash of the calendar" issues? (i.e., Pentecost vs. Memorial Day, Sunday in Easter vs. Mother's Day, Catechetical or Vocation Sunday, etc.)

- What is going on in the lives of the parish community? In the country? In the world?

2. Begin with prayer (including silence).

Once the group has gathered together, it is essential to begin with prayer. This should not be seen as perfunctory; the preparation team should genuinely work in an atmosphere of prayer and reflection, calling upon God to guide their time together. Some sample prayers are offered in Appendix B for the team to utilize, but feel free to develop your own approach.

3. Evaluate the previous Sunday's celebration.

Evaluation is important. Good notes should be taken, and the discussion should be honest and forthright; otherwise it can be reduced to an exercise of self-congratulation. This should not take up too much time, but it should not be ignored either. Also, this should not be purely "what did I like or not like" but a discussion during which the team can offer solid critiques and reflections.

4. Reading, reflection, and faith sharing with the Scripture readings.

It is important to remember that the Scripture readings appointed for the celebration provide the primary path for the preparation process. As pastoral musicians and liturgical leaders, this is a challenge for all of us to be more biblically literate. This step in the process is essentially the centerpiece for this model of preparation. A member of the team carefully and prayerfully reads the Gospel selection appointed for the celebration. The rest of the team should take part in true active listening (not taking notes). This should be done reflectively, and there should not be any reading along in a missalette or Lectionary by the other team members. This is very important. Listening and *experiencing* the reading is the challenge here, and the preparation team should try

Part 3: A 10-Step Process for Liturgical Preparation

to resist the temptation to become task-oriented at this point. Rather, they should allow and treat themselves to just "drink in" the power and richness of the Word. A good, intentional silence follows (again, without note taking).

Then, a *different* member of the team reads the exact same Gospel selection a second time. A different voice, with a change of timbre, provides the team with a fresh rendering of the reading. This time, other members of the team may want to take notes as they listen, focusing on key words, striking phrases, or images heard in the reading. Again, this is *not* an inventory of "what songs to use" or anything else geared toward the specific task. Rather, the focus of the reflection here is: what in the reading (words, phrase, or image) provokes, touches, and speaks to the heart. Faith sharing then begins among the members of the team. Once again, the temptation is to head right into filling out a planning sheet, shouting out song ideas, and so forth. Try to avoid the rush to complete the task, and stay centered in faith sharing. For those of you who may be new to faith sharing in such a setting, it is important to see this as a time of personal sharing that always leads back to the more communal concerns of the parish community. How is the Word sparking conversion and faith? How might it be speaking to the parish community? While theological or doctrinal insights often rise to the surface in such a discussion (and they should certainly not be suppressed), the intention of this time is *not* to engage in theological debate.

Repeat this exact process (a reading by two different members of the team) with the First Reading (usually from the Old Testament, or Hebrew scriptures). This reading traditionally has a very strong connection with the Gospel proclamation. As before, discussion and faith sharing on this reading takes place, along with recognizing connections and similarities found with the Gospel reading. At this point, it is good to begin to develop a "focus" (remember, not a "theme") found in the scriptures. This is where a good commentary can help to bring some sense of the intent of the biblical authors, moving beyond "what *I* think the scripture means." When we have a deeper understanding of the original context, it provides a more corrective theology and pastoral dimension of the Word.[3] Then members of the team can reference the Second Reading, which sometimes, but not always, may have a strong connection to the other readings. The Responsorial Psalm is also a rich resource for reflection (and, unfortunately, often ignored in liturgical planning), and the team should really pour over this text, which is often a pastoral and human reflection upon the other lectionary readings of the day. For music ministers, reflection and study of the psalm text should be a priority.[4]

After a while, the personal faith sharing of the team should shift its focus toward the community who will be gathering together to celebrate. The questions that come to the surface at this point are: What are the scriptures attempting to proclaim to the Church at large? What are they attempting to say to our particular parish community? From these questions, try to formulate a *central question* (often referred to as "the question of the week") for the homilist to pose and share during the homily. Here we find the beginnings of homily content, musical choices, and—very important—ongoing catechesis, formation, and reflection throughout the week that follows in all the activities and programs in the parish.[5]

5. Look at some of the other ritual texts.

The team then should look at the assigned Opening Prayer (Collect) of the liturgical celebration found in the Sacramentary. This Opening Prayer is often a good "summing up" of the focus that is revealed in the Word. The same is true for the Communion Antiphon, the Prayer over the Gifts, and the Prayer after Communion. These texts are often ignored, yet they provide a richness that can help to reveal and shape the image of the liturgy.

6. Reveal the relationship to the season.

The next step is to see how this specific liturgical celebration fits in the context of the journey through the liturgical year. How do the biblical and ritual texts appointed for this liturgy relate to the specific and/or overall liturgical season?

7. Begin to be attentive to the specific "ritual units" found in the liturgy.

As stated before, the many specific and final ritual decisions would be determined after the meeting. However, the team can begin to explore and ask some questions for consideration about the ritual content.

Gathering Rites: Because the Gathering Rites are intended to bring a diverse group of people into a unified, prayerful, and attentive community, the team needs to reflect on how the people gather through hospitality and intentional interaction with each other. The beginning of the celebration should actually embody the focus and intent of the Word. Is the mood joyful or somber? Praise-centered or penitential in nature? Do pieces of music come to mind? What ritual creativity is possible? Decisions regarding use of Penitential Rite, Gloria, and Sprinkling need to take place here, as well as questions around the ritual "choreography." Will there be a procession? What are the primary symbols?

The Word: Return to the Liturgy of the Word and consider how the assembly can participate and respond to what they have heard. What about the Gospel Acclamation? Would a procession of the Book of the Gospels be appropriate? Should we use incense during the acclamation? Should the intercessions be sung or recited? Are we tying the message of the Word into the content of these petitions? Other creative ritual questions come to mind at this point, such as how can the homily be a more participatory experience for and with the assembly? Could the homily include a sung refrain that echoes the message in the preaching? These and other related issues should be discussed.

The Meal: There are many possibilities for consideration here. Should the Preparation of the Gifts and the setting of the table be simple, or more elaborate? Should we have the assembly sing at this point, or would a selection featuring the choir, instrumental music, or even silence be more appropriate and effective? Which Eucharistic Prayer text would be most suitable for the occasion? Is there a particular preface that would best echo the Word for this celebration? Should the Prayer be sung? What song would best accompany the sharing of communion? The communion song should be focused on meal sharing but at the same time support the message of the Word for this celebration. After the sharing of communion is over, would a communal hymn of thanksgiving be appropriate?

Sending Forth: The overwhelming consideration is mission: How are we sending the community forth to more deeply *live* the Word proclaimed and preached today? How can the meal that has been shared be enshrined by our considerations of the final blessing or a song of sending forth? What should happen ritually to engage the assembly to this mission?

8. Begin to make some specific choices.

This can happen in many different ways, and the unique pastoral setting would determine how and who makes the more specific choices. Some of the final decisions can take place at the meeting or after the meeting is concluded. In most cases, specific final choices of music need to be made by the music minister, but other members of the team should feel free to make suggestions and offer ideas. Remember to utilize the excellent biblical, liturgical, and seasonal indexes in hymnals such as *Gather Comprehensive—Second Edition* and *RitualSong* (both published by GIA Publications, Inc.), which can provide direction for musical choices. The presider and/or homilist would hopefully take some time with the team at this point to surface and summarize the key areas of focus (or formulate a "question of the week") shared with the participants in their faith sharing in order to incorporate its breadth into the homily.

9. Summarize by asking some basic questions.

After all of the different considerations and ideas have begun to take shape, ask some basic and concrete questions:

- What are our hopes for this celebration?
- How is the Paschal Mystery (dying and rising with and in Christ) being celebrated and proclaimed in this celebration?
- Ultimately, what will this celebration proclaim about God, faith, and the Church?

10. End with prayer.

At the end of the meeting, it is good to come back to the source and surrender all of the deliberations to God's hands and direction.

After the meeting is over, the presider or homilist should use ideas from the meeting to develop the homily. Similarly, the minister of music should consider the ideas presented alongside the real constraints of what is familiar to the choirs, cantors, ensembles, and the community, as well as the balance of time needed to prepare. The music minister will hopefully reflect upon the faith sharing and insights, and then agonize over the final choices that need to be made. Together, these elements are brought together in the final design of the ritual, not necessarily with the preparation team but by the primary leaders of the liturgy (presider, musician, liturgist, etc.).

Finally, all of the ministers and leaders should rehearse well. Then—let go—and celebrate the liturgy!

… To Worship in Spirit and Truth

Notes:

1. Obviously, when preparing the more complex rituals and celebrations of Christmas, the Easter Triduum (Holy Thursday, Good Friday, and the Easter Vigil) and other sacramental celebrations (such as the many rituals of the RCIA), this would require a more involved process, resulting in the need for more time.
2. Appendix C provides several excellent lectionary commentaries to utilize in this regard.
3. The importance for liturgical musicians to engage in some kind of biblical study cannot be overemphasized because it is foundational and parallel to their musical and liturgical development. While taking a biblical theology class may not be possible, there are many excellent resources available for personal reading and study. Appendix C provides many suggestions.
4. A singular and excellent kind of resource for examining the depths of the responsorial psalms as they appear in the Lectionary and the Liturgical Year is *Sing a New Song: The Psalms in the Sunday Lectionary* by Irene Nowell, OSB (Collegeville: Liturgical Press). This book is a must have for pastoral musicians, for cantors in particular.
5. A most recent and prophetic movement and concept that truly weds the worlds of liturgy and catechesis is well articulated in Bill Huebsch's book, *Whole Community Catechesis in Plain English* (Mystic, CT: Twenty Third Publications). Pastoral musicians, liturgists, and homilists need to read and delve into this book, and see the connections made between the homily, the worship of the Sunday assembly, and the weekly aspects of parish life. At the center of the homiletic and catechetical connection is the development of the "question of the week": a focus for the community to ponder and reflect upon after their dismissal from the liturgical celebration.

Postlude

Embracing this approach is a risk, but one that is worthwhile. This paradigm shift requires a leap of faith because it is so different from the way liturgical preparation is usually done. Many who are reading this may feel that it is simply too hard and too much work, and will choose to stay with what is safe and familiar. While this is understandable, a serious challenge is placed before us to not dismiss the need for some sort of process centered in prayer and Scripture, in which the overall liturgical and pastoral considerations are at the center of our choices. There is no question that adopting this or a similar process requires a commitment of time and energy, so it is important to start slowly and gently, fashioning this approach to your particular situation. There will be minor bumps along the way, but our parish celebrations deserve such attentiveness and hard work. There are too many of us in liturgical and pastoral music leadership who unfortunately work in isolation because the parish priest or other leaders reject the need to collaborate and surrender themselves to such a process. Even if the pastor or others cannot or will not participate, the challenge is clear for us to develop and commit to some sort of process similar to the one presented here, centered in the Word, prayer, and the deep structures of the rite, one who pays careful attention to the people in our parish communities.

Of course, planning alone, just picking songs and filling in the blanks is easier, less complicated, and probably more "efficient." Many of us like working alone because there is no one to disagree with us. Pastoral music leaders now work in a time when there are numerous magazines and liturgical planning software programs available that provide "recipes" and listings directing us as to which pieces of music to use. These resources are popular because they make planning easier for us. We can fall into a perception that these magazines and planning programs can do the work for us. Good liturgy is not, nor should it be, that easy. Obviously, the support offered from these magazines and technologies is helpful, but they should be supplementary, used as secondary resources. When periodicals and Internet resources are the primary influences that drive our choices and process, authentic celebration is severely compromised. The primary resources for parish worship are the deep ritual structures already present: the Word and the lives and gifts shared by the community. Certainly, final choices and specific decisions need to be made by the liturgical leaders. At the same time, we need to participate in a prayerful and collaborative process in which our decisions are grounded in the spiritual lives of the community from a place of service and surrender rather than simply imposing our personal tastes and opinions. High-quality and collaborative preparation that honors the community and keeps them at the center of our concern will help to nurture a communal life of prayer more in keeping with our call.

Our vocation is to empower a participatory and communal celebration, supported by a ministry of music that is truly the prayer and praise of the worshiping assembly. Our call in this ministry is to know and deepen our relationship with Christ and to help make Christ known to those who gather to pray. When we do so, we can be transformed to become the mystical and musical Body of Christ.

Take the risk. The people of God certainly deserve it, and our liturgy and prayer will be the better for it. May God bless you all in this most important ministry.

Soli Deo Gloria!

Appendix A
The Structure of the Eucharist

Structure of the Rite

GATHERING
Hospitality
Preparation of the Assembly
Song of Gathering *
Greeting
Sprinkling Rite **
Penitential Rite *
Glory to God **
Opening Prayer

WORD
Hebrew Scripture Reading
Responsorial Psalm **
Christian Scripture Reading
Gospel Acclamation **
Gospel Proclamation
Homily

Spirituality of the Rite

MANY BECOMING ONE
Forming the community

Opening statement of faith

The community focuses

TELLING THE STORIES
Telling the ancestral story
Icon(s) for the total Word
Telling more of the story
Praising the Word alive
Telling the Good News
Preaching the Good News

Appendix A: Structure of the Eucharist

Special Rites (occasionally)
Profession of Faith   Stating our beliefs
General Intercessions *   Praying for the world

TABLE   **ACTING AND THANKING
                                              IN MEMORY OF CHRIST**

Preparation of the Table and Gifts *   Preparing gifts (us, money, bread,
                                              and wine)

Prayer over the Gifts
Eucharistic Prayer   Blessing, praising, giving thanks
Preface
First Eucharistic Acclamation: Holy, Holy **
Epiclesis
Narrative of the Institution
Second Eucharistic Acclamation:
    Memorial Acclamation **
Intercessory Prayer
Third Eucharistic Acclamation:
    Doxology/Amen**
The Communion Rite   Sharing the meal
The Lord's Prayer*   Praying as Jesus taught
The Sign of Peace   Extending community
The Breaking of the Bread: Lamb of God**   Breaking and pouring
The Communion Sharing: Table Song **   Becoming the Body of Christ
Hymn/Song of Thanksgiving*   Thanking God for gifts
Prayer After Communion   Summing it up

GOING FORTH   **BEING THE BODY OF LIFE**
Announcements   Being Church
Final Blessing*   Going forth to love and serve
Song of Mission*
* *can be sung*   ** *is always sung*

Copyright © 2001 The Emmaus Center for Music, Prayer, and Ministry.
Used with permission. All rights reserved.

Appendix B
Prayers for the Preparation Process

Prayer Before Preparing a Celebration

God,
You are wonderful and great
and you fill us with joy!

We ask that you center our hearts
and our thoughts,
as we humbly encounter your Word.
May your spirit of wisdom come to us
as we make the many choices
to help make your presence—
which is always here—
become more real for your people.

Bless this time, and instill in us
a spirit of prayerful preparation.
May our decisions be transformed
into a celebration proclaiming You,
breaking forth among us!

Come to us now.
Amen.

*(by David Haas, from With Every Note I Sing, © 1995
GIA Publications, Inc. All rights reserved. Used with permission.)*

Prayer and Song for Centering, Sharing and Reflecting on the Word of God

Open Our Minds

Open our minds to know you, Lord;
Open our ears to hear your voice;
Open our hearts now to your Word;
Come to us now, O Lord, our God.
This prayer may be sung to the tune of "Praise God from Whom All Blessings Flow."

*(by David Haas, from With Every Note I Sing, © 1995
GIA Publications, Inc. All rights reserved. Used with permission.)*

To Worship in Spirit and Truth

Come Now, O Word of God

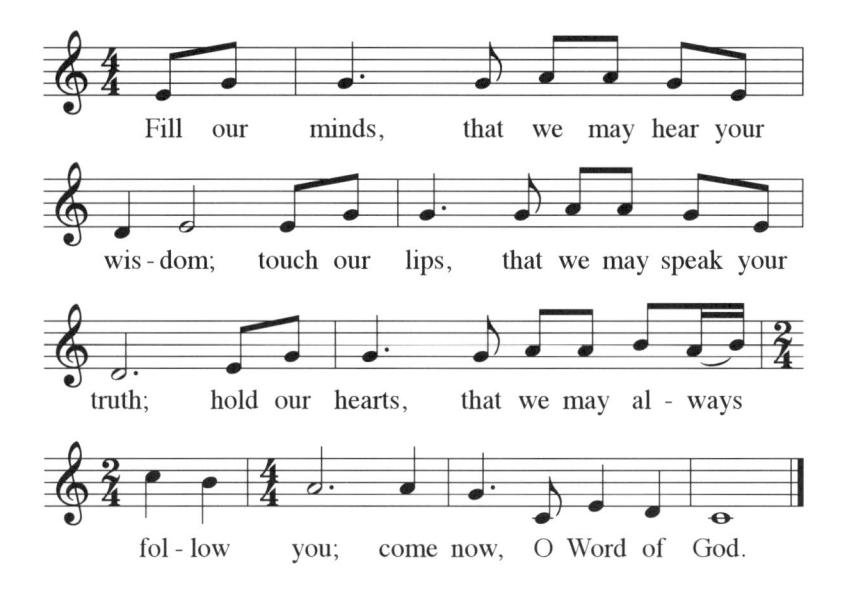

Fill our minds, that we may hear your wis-dom; touch our lips, that we may speak your truth; hold our hearts, that we may al-ways fol-low you; come now, O Word of God.

*(by David Haas, from We Give You Thanks, © 1997
GIA Publications, Inc. All rights reserved. Used with permission.)*

Appendix C

Resources for Further Reading and Study

Foundational Liturgical Documents and Guides

A Guide to the General Instruction of the Roman Missal, Paul Turner (Liturgy Training Publications, Chicago, 2003)

The Catechism of the Catholic Church on Liturgy and Sacraments, Jan Michael Joncas (Resource Publications, San Jose, 1995)

The General Instruction of the Roman Missal, 1969–2002: A Commentary, Dennis C. Smolarski (The Liturgical Press, Collegeville, 2003)

The Liturgy Documents: A Parish Resource, Vol. 1 (Fourth Edition) (Liturgy Training Publications, Chicago, 2004)

The Liturgy Documents: A Parish Resource, Vol. 2 (Liturgy Training Publications, Chicago, 2000)

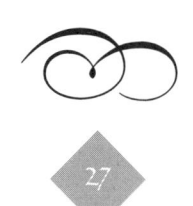

Liturgical Preparation and Planning

Lectionary for Mass: Study Edition
(Liturgy Training Publications, Chicago, 1999)

Liturgy Made Simple: A Theology and Spirituality, Mark Searle (The Liturgical Press, Collegeville, 1981)

Preparing for Liturgy, Austin Fleming (Liturgy Training Publications, Chicago, 1997)

The Eucharist: Essence, Form, Celebration (Second Edition), Johannes H. Emminghaus (The Liturgical Press, Collegeville, 1997)

Living Liturgy (Zimmerman, Harmon, et al; The Liturgical Press, Collegeville, annual publication)

Sourcebook for Sundays and Seasons: An Almanac of Parish Liturgy (Liturgy Training Publications, Chicago, annual publication)

Q & A: The Mass, Dennis C. Smolarski (Liturgy Training Publications, Chicago, 2002)

Sunday Mass Five Years from Now, Gabe Huck (Liturgy Training Publications, Chicago, 2001)

How Not to Say Mass: A Guidebook on Liturgical Principles and the Roman Missal, Dennis C. Smolarski (Paulist Press, New York, 2003)

Forming the Assembly to Celebrate the Mass, Lawrence E. Mick (Liturgy Training Publications, Chicago, 2001)

Forming the Assembly to Celebrate Sacraments, Lawrence E. Mick (Liturgy Training Publications, Chicago, 2002)

Disputed Questions in the Liturgy Today, John M. Huels (Liturgy Training Publications, Chicago, 1988)

More Disputed Questions in the Liturgy Today, John M. Huels (Liturgy Training Publications, Chicago, 1996)

Modern Liturgy Answers the 101 Most-Asked Questions About Liturgy, Nick Wagner (Resource Publications, San Jose, 1996)

Catechesis for Liturgy: A Program for Parish Involvement, Gilbert Ostdiek (The Pastoral Press/OCP Publications, Portland, 1986)

The Book of Sacramental Basics, Tad W. Guzie (Paulist Press, New York, 1982)

Making Parish Policy: A Workbook on Sacramental Policies, Ron Lewinski (Liturgy Training Publications, Chicago, 1996)

LiturgyHelp.com (Liturgical Planning Software Resource) (GIA Publications, Inc., Chicago)

Lectionary Commentaries

Preaching the New Lectionary (Three Volumes), Diane Bergant (The Liturgical Press, Collegeville, 2000)

The Word We Celebrate: Commentary on the Sunday Lectionary, Years A, B, and C, Patricia Datchuck Sanchez (Sheed and Ward, Kansas City, 1989)

Days of the Lord (several volumes) (The Liturgical Press, Collegeville, 1991)

The Word Embodied: Meditations on the Sunday Scriptures (Cycle A), John F. Kavanaugh (Orbis, Maryknoll, 1998)

The Word Encountered: Meditations on the Sunday Scriptures (Cycle B), John F. Kavanaugh (Orbis, Maryknoll, 1996)

The Word Engaged: Meditations on the Sunday Scriptures (Cycle C), John F. Kavanaugh (Orbis, Maryknoll, 1997)

Sing A New Song: The Psalms in the Sunday Lectionary, Irene Nowell, OSB (The Liturgical Press, Collegeville, 1993)

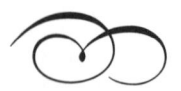

Other Scripture Resources

The Collegeville Bible Commentary: Based on the New American Bible, Diane Bergant, Robert J. Karris, editors (The Liturgical Press, Collegeville, 1992)

Reading the Old Testament: An Introduction, Lawrence Boadt (Paulist Press, New York, 1984)

The Writings of the New Testament: An Interpretation (Revised Edition), Luke Timothy Johnson (Augsburg Fortress, Minneapolis, 1999)

The Message of the Psalms: A Theological Commentary, Walter Brueggemann (Augsburg Fortress, Minneapolis, 1984)

Tell Me Your Name: Images of God in the Bible, Arthur E. Zannoni (Liturgy Training Publications, Chicago, 2000)

Tell Me Your Story: The Parables of Jesus, Arthur E. Zannoni (Liturgy Training Publications, Chicago, 2002)

Dining in the Kingdom of God: The Origins of the Eucharist in the Gospel of Luke, Eugene LaVerdiere (Liturgy Training Publications, Chicago, 1994)

The Breaking of the Bread: The Development of the Eucharist According to Acts, Eugene LaVerdiere (Liturgy Training Publications, Chicago, 1997)

Reading the Bible Again for the First Time: Taking the Bible Seriously But Not Literally, Marcus J. Borg (Harper, San Francisco, 2001)

Liturgical Music Resources

Gather Comprehensive—Second Edition (several editions) (GIA Publications, Inc., Chicago)

RitualSong (several editions) (GIA Publications, Inc., Chicago)

Hymns for the Gospels, A hymnal supplement, W. Thomas Smith, Robert J. Batastini, editors (GIA Publications, Inc., Chicago)

Lead Me, Guide Me (GIA Publications, Inc., Chicago)

Worship—Third Edition (GIA Publications, Inc., Chicago)

JourneySongs (OCP Publications, Portland)

Peoples Mass Book (World Library Publications, Schiller Park)

Music and the Mass: A Practical Guide for Ministers of Music, David Haas (Liturgy Training Publications, Chicago, 1998)

Visions of Liturgy and Music for a New Century, Lucien Deiss (The Liturgical Press, Collegeville, 1996)

The Heart of the Matter, Paul Westermeyer (GIA Publications, Inc., Chicago, 2001)

The Ministry and Mission of Sung Prayer, David Haas (Saint Anthony Messenger Press, Cincinnati, 2002)

From Sacred Song to Ritual Music: Twentieth-Century Understandings of Roman Catholic Worship Music, Jan Michael Joncas (The Liturgical Press, Collegeville, 1997)

The Liturgical Music Answer Book, Peggy Lovrien (Resource Publications, San Jose, 1999)

The GIA Quarterly (quarterly magazine), Fred Moleck, editor (GIA Publications, Inc., Chicago)

Pastoral Music (bimonthly magazine), Gordon Truitt, editor (The National Association of Pastoral Musicians, Silver Spring, MD)

Ministry and Liturgy (magazine), Donna Cole, editor (Resource Publications, San Jose)

With Every Note I Sing (Prayers for Music Ministers and Those Who Love to Sing), David Haas (GIA Publications, Inc., Chicago, 1995)

I Will Sing Forever (More Prayers for Music Ministers and Those Who Love to Sing), David Haas (GIA Publications, Inc., Chicago, 2001)

The Milwaukee Symposia for Church Composers: A Ten Year Report, Ed Foley and Gabe Huck, editors (Liturgy Training Publications, Chicago, 1992)

Relationship of Liturgy, Catechesis, and Parish Life

Whole Community Catechesis in Plain English, Bill Huebsch (Twenty-Third Publications, Mystic, CT, 2002)

Handbook for Success in Whole Community Catechesis, Bill Huebsch (Twenty-Third Publications, Mystic, CT, 2003)

Increase Our Faith: Prayer Services and Faith Sharing for Whole Community Catechesis, David Haas (Twenty-Third Publications, Mystic, CT, and GIA Publications, Inc., Chicago, 2004)

Bringing Liturgy and Catechesis Together: Let the Mystery Lead You!, Joe Paprocki and D. Todd Williamson (Twenty-Third Publications, Mystic, CT, 2002)

Here Comes Everybody: Whole Community Catechesis in the Parish, Leisa Anslinger (Twenty-Third Publications, Mystic, CT, 2004)

Introducing Liturgical Catechesis: Formation Sessions for the Parish, Nick Wagner (Resource Publications, San Jose, 2002)

Word and Worship Workbook: For Ministry in Initiation, Preaching, Religious Education and Formation (separate volumes for Cycles A, B, and C), Mary Birmingham (Paulist Press, New York)